The Digital Trifecta

Frank Mazza
Steven Ziegler

Copyright © 2021 Frank Mazza.
All rights reserved.
ISBN: 9798528967462

DEDICATION

To my wife and children who bring me the ultimate success.

CONTENTS

	Introduction	i
1	Hustle & History	1
2	LinkedIn	5
3	Email	10
4	Facebook	20
5	The Digital Trifecta & You	40
6	Fostering the Relationship	43
7	A Universal Solution	46

Introduction

I could not tell you how many times I considered writing a book but felt like the timing just wasn't right. For me, reading is never a hobby; it is always about finding a few gems that I could implement into my career and build upon. So, when COVID-19 hit, the world of digital was changing, small businesses needed help, and I finally felt like the time was now.

Let's get this part out of the way first. I do not put myself on the same level as my business inspirations who are the likes of the late Steve Jobs, Elon Musk, and Mark Cuban…. mentally I do…. but I am still on the horse riding strong and creating my own pathway to success. This book is coming from a person who, like every entrepreneur, is still creating their footprint. The book is meant to share the secrets that I have used to help primarily B2B companies find immediate growth. These are NOT proprietary secrets, rather my trial and error sort of research obtained from working with companies globally and developing a solution to make them all work together (The Digital Trifecta).

When reading this book, you will realize that I kept everything straight to the point and in a simplified version. I want you to read this book the way I like to read: skip ahead and find the value, use it as a reference guide, make it look good on your bookshelf until you're ready or become extremely interested and never drop it until you're finished. I won't judge your way of reading this as long as I can get to my goal. I want you to find one or two things that you can implement for yourself or your business. If this happens, then I did my job in presenting you with something worthwhile.

To ensure I was able to bring value to you, I brought in support from another like-minded entrepreneur, Steven Ziegler. Steven is a fundraising professional with over a decade of experience in the non-profit vertical. Steven and I connected about eight years ago when he wrote the script for a short-film that we worked on together. He has played a huge part in ensuring that my thoughts and writing would be presented in a way that will provide you value.

Hate it or love it, I would love to hear your feedback and ideas. Please feel free to email me at: feedback@frankmazza.net. Also don't hesitate to share your review and a photo of the book on social media (hopefully it's 5 stars!).

Enjoy.

1 Hustle & History

Prior to writing this book, I have remained behind the scenes for more than thirteen years of my professional career. I have led various digital marketing strategies leveraging products, mobile applications, and B2B marketing. I currently hold over twenty licenses and certifications relating to digital transformation, analytics, and social media. I have consulted globally with over fifty companies, including one of the largest printer manufacturers in Japan and a prominent healthcare technology company in India. I would consider myself a bit of a digital scientist, as I have been willing to digitally experiment with just about everything.

There has never been a more challenging or rewarding time to be in the business of marketing and selling technology to businesses. I take pride in understanding new and dynamically changing industries of all shapes and sizes through digital strategies. My ultimate goal is to bring out the best in companies with the least amount of spend possible. The Digital Trifecta works and much of this book will show you why through the use of statistics, data, and process. These elements of success are learned in classrooms and offices, but there is also an intangible that will make your business thrive: hustle.

For me, hustling was in the blood. My late grandfather, Francesco Augustine Mazza Sr., was an Italian immigrant who began chasing his American Dream of entrepreneurship in the 1930's. Immediately upon his arrival in America, he began shining shoes to help provide for his family of ten. He later transitioned to street vending, which he built into a very successful business. My father eventually took that business over and scaled it to new levels. He always said to me, "I do this to make sure you never have to." In my early childhood, I learned how to sell products. Hot dogs, pretzels, and t-shirts helped to pay my college tuition. My father understood his customers. He taught me about supply and demand, and more importantly, how to convert new customers faster than any billboard or high-priced advertisement could do. Failure was never an option for my lineage of entrepreneurs, and neither would it be for me.

In 2010, I graduated from college. The Great Recession was over, and I was on the hunt for a job. Constant rejection was physically and mentally exhausting. Countless interviews left me with a feeling of defeat and when I landed a job as an entry level marketing manager, I almost did not take it. The feeling of defeat lingered as I was thinking, "I just graduated college and the best I can do is $12.50 an hour?" But, I remembered what it meant to hustle. This was a new way of doing it. After contemplating my next steps, I decided to use this experience as an opportunity to learn more about digital and keep exploring my options.

Prior to graduation, communication courses in higher education were in the early stages of understanding the importance of new digital platforms. I was exposed to LinkedIn for the first time. While the business was already seven years old, it had just reached the general public. I saw the opportunities for personal and professional growth. I began building my network and connecting with the appropriate people. That $12.50 an hour job? I landed the interview through LinkedIn.

I experienced success on LinkedIn and was beginning to get noticed. In just two months, I saw that the platform was more than a job board, it was a way to build a business and my reputation. Through research and messaging, I was able to earn freelance design jobs for professional athletes, television personalities, and multiple businesses around the globe. I hustled and sent over twenty messages daily. My technology day-job gave me the freedom to explore the digital space and encouraged the use of LinkedIn. It worked. I dominated the limousine industry as the marketing contact for 15 companies nationally. My favorite was the company "Heaven on Wheels," which recently gained publicity for creating a custom vehicle to drive Joe Exotic home, had he been pardoned.

Word of mouth, networking, traditional marketing, email prospecting, and social media promotion have their place in business. They also represent progression and innovation in the modern world. From John Wanamaker pondering which half of his advertising dollars were wasted to Jeff Bezos creating unique customer profiles, business magnates will forever ask the question, "How much is the customer worth?"

The customer is everything. Translating that to sales is the final step in a cultivation process that can be calculated without being cold. You can build natural relationships with your customers that rely on trust and discovering solutions. You can be organized and authentic. You can customize the process, drive more sales, and create more opportunities along the way. This is the Digital Trifecta. The Trifecta consists of three components that are at your disposal: LinkedIn, Email, and Facebook. With these assets, you can pace your business in the modern world. These are the tools that will tap into your entrepreneurial spirit and unleash your hustle.

2 LinkedIn

LinkedIn is where I began, so it is only fitting that the Digital Trifecta begins with understanding this colossal networking tool.

LinkedIn began in 2003 as a professional networking tool. In 2021, the platform hosts 740 million users from 150 countries. By using the platform to search for people in your field or those who could benefit from your services, you will find endless opportunities. I am a big believer in the power of LinkedIn. Like any social media company or commerce website in the modern era, LinkedIn uses your information to generate ad revenue. However, I see this as a tradeoff for being able to craft a personal brand and build an audience from a micro perspective. The personal information garnered from LinkedIn also builds the algorithm that narrows down your most pertinent prospects. Research is made easier, but it is not done for you. You must be willing to initiate contact. This requires confidence. Everyone has a different comfort level in this respect, but with the knowledge you are gaining to navigate the digital space, you may be surprised to learn how many people in your orbit will welcome your initiative.

Start your LinkedIn search based on

industry. If you are in the technology industry and work for a CRM company and you are looking to find a Chief Technology Officer (CTO), Chief Information Officer (CIO), or the Chief Marketing Officer (CMO) of a potential client, use the search portal to find these people and their companies. No matter the industry or the number of acronyms, the process remains the same. I encourage you to align with the LinkedIn limits and connect with the 50 people in your industry daily. This research and outreach should take one hour and can be built into your daily routine.

After you connect, the next step is the introduction. Because of the LinkedIn algorithm, it is best not to do this immediately. Once your connection is accepted, LinkedIn will provide you with the best opportunity to send the message by notifying you that the connection has been made manually. When that occurs, send one short paragraph introducing yourself, your product, and your business. By connecting and messaging you have already achieved two touch points. More touch points in the first month set the stage for continued growth throughout the Trifecta. This is why you should continue to share content related to your industry or product daily, along with the outreach. The more you share on LinkedIn, the more potential prospect touchpoints.

Examples of messages following your connection

Direct Message #1 — *The Initial Outreach*

It is critical to keep the first message short. Less is more, as most people will typically ignore that extremely long email. This should be sent following the acceptance of your new connection. Feel free to customize.

Hey [First Name]!

Hope all is well! Not sure if you are aware but the company I am with, [Company Name], has a product that I believe is a perfect fit for your company. Let me know if you have a few minutes to learn more, and I will send you the details.

- [Your Name]

Direct Message Example #2 —
Responding to The No Response

Message #2 should be sent if they don't respond to the first message. It should provide more information about your product or service, but not be as long as a novel! Feel free to add video links, or links to presentations. This message should be sent 3-5 days following the initial outreach.

[First Name] —

Just wanted to quickly follow-up on my previous message. My company [Company Name] has a product that I believe is a perfect fit for your company. Below are a few links to videos that I have put together to help share more insight. Let me know if you have a few minutes to discuss.

Here is a link to [Video Title]: [Link 1]

Here is a link to [Video Title]: [Link 2]

- [Your Name]

Direct Message Example #3 — *The Response Follow-up*

Great news! They responded, hopefully they are interested! This message should be sent immediately following the response. Keep this short, as your goal is to get a phone number or email to schedule a call.

Thanks [First Name]!

Let me know a good number/email where I can reach you. Below are a few links to videos that I have put together to help share more insight before our call:

Here is a link to [Video Title]: [Link 1]

Here is a link to [Video Title]: [Link 2]

- [Your Name]

3 E-MAIL

In practice, the Digital Trifecta relies on email to bridge the gap between LinkedIn and Facebook. Email remains the most practical form of communication in the modern world. Acquiring the correct email address for your business purposes is essential to converting your contacts to customers.

The average open rate for emails is 15-25% while the average click-through rate is 2.5%. Your average click-to-open rate should be between 20-30%. These numbers illustrate why building your contact database through at least 50 daily LinkedIn connections is vital to your eventual revenue generation. Do not be discouraged by the seemingly low percentages mentioned above. With the right plan, email can easily generate 25-35% of your revenue. (CampaignMonitor.com)

Because various digital platforms serve different purposes (i.e. LinkedIn for business, Facebook for personal interests, etc.,) each connection is likely to be using multiple email addresses. But, if you can acquire at least one, you will be making progress. Depending on your business plan and comfortability, you may want to consider an additional, slightly less organic option to gather information. One of my favorite tools for this type of endeavor is SalesQL. This tool allows you to gather information from LinkedIn, add it to your own CRM, and connect with various email marketing platforms such as MailChimp, Constant Contact, or HubSpot, to name a few. It will also validate potential contact information of your prospect such as company, email, and phone numbers.

To optimize the Digital Trifecta, streamline the process of reaching your contacts on multiple platforms. The LinkedIn step of messaging your new contacts will lead to success through email. While SalesQL is a helpful tool, messaging allows for organic connections to grow. As you foster a relationship with the CTO, CIO, or CMO, you will go beyond the business stream. When it is time to introduce yourself to your 50 new contacts each day, you will prove that you are legitimate, and you can also begin building your database with the information available on LinkedIn. As the conversation builds and you each begin to disclose more to one another, you will gather more information. It is permissible to ask for their preferred email to continue the conversation beyond LinkedIn. This will help populate your database and make your email campaigns more effective.

I cannot stress enough the importance of the LinkedIn conversation. Your professional photo, company, title, and anything else you have chosen to showcase is available to your new contact and proves that you are human. When you begin the email campaign, it will be well received by your new network. The personal aspect and the hustle of Part 1 of the Digital Trifecta is all preparation for the automation of Part 2.

In my experience, email contact with your potential new customer will be most successful if you appear in their inbox six times in the first month. The more you touch the contact, the better your opportunity. Your first email should be another introduction. Remind them you connected on LinkedIn and that you would like to set up a call. Import your data from LinkedIn to your database on a bi-weekly basis. Keeping to this schedule will allow you to build your growing campaign and give some breathing room to your new contact. You will continue increasing the number of email addresses in your database while perfecting the content of your emails and your product pitch.

Sample Drip Timeline

Day One – Initial email
Day Two – Follow Up
Day Seven – Advertisement
Day Fourteen – Advertisement
Day Thirty – Advertisement
Day Thirty-One – Re-introduction

When your emails are working, you can shift the style that your new connection is receiving as they have remained opted-in and interested in your brand. If you do not acquire new business in the first month, stay committed. Do not get discouraged. The drip campaign will continue for an entire year with a total of 16 emails.

While the email campaign is automated, the hustle does not stop. Connecting with 50 people daily will, in theory, bring 1,550 new contacts to your database each month. You are going to use their information to create your custom Facebook audience. With your tools like SalesQL and Legion, you can match your email database to Facebook. You will not have a 100% total match, but even a 25-50% match will provide you with up to 500 prospects who will know your business and recognize your brand the more you continue to strategically make yourself more visible. The final step of the Digital Trifecta is a hybrid of personalization and automation.

(Tip: Be sure to include your name or the name of a sales associate on your team in all emails, ads, and digital branding of your product to reassure your connections of your belief in your products.)

Email Samples.

The next few pages are some examples of automated emails that I have seen huge success with and in many cases exceeded the open and click-through-rates.

[DAY ONE – INITIAL EMAIL]

Hi [First Name]!

Hope all is well! We recently connected on LinkedIn and not sure if you are aware but [Company Name], has a product that I believe is a perfect fit for your company? Let me know if you have a few minutes to learn more. I can send you the details.

Thanks,
[Your Name]
[Contact Information]

[DAY TWO – FOLLOW UP]

Hi [First Name]!

Hope all is well! Just wanted to follow-up on my previous email. We recently connected on LinkedIn and not sure if you are aware but [Company Name], has a product that I believe is a perfect fit for your company. Let me know if you have a few minutes to learn more, I can send you the details.

Thanks,
[Your Name]
[Contact Information]

[DAY SEVEN – ADVERTISEMENT]

Hi [First Name]!

Did you know we can help your business grow with our product [Product Name]?

Here is a link to [Video Title]: [Link 1]

Here is a link to [Video Title]: [Link 2]

Let me know if you have a few minutes to learn more, I can send you the details.

Thanks,
[Your Name]
[Contact Information]

[DAY FOURTEEN – ADVERTISEMENT]

Hi [First Name]!

Let [Company Name] help your business grow with our product [Product Name]? [Product Description]

Here is a link to [Video Title]: [Link 1]

Here is a link to [Video Title]: [Link 2]

Let me know if you have a few minutes to learn more.

Thanks,
[Your Name]
[Contact Information]

[DAY THIRTY – ADVERTISEMENT]

Hi [First Name]!

Our Product, [Product Name] is helping companies see immediate growth in revenue! [Product Description]

See for yourself! [Link 1]

Let me know if you have a few minutes to learn more. Does next *Tuesday* at 2 PM work for you?

Thanks,
[Your Name]
[Contact Information]

[DAY THIRTY-ONE – RE-INTRODUCTION]

Hi [First Name]!

It's been a while since we last connected! Wanted to send you a quick reminder that we can help your business grow with our product [Product Name]? [Product Description]

Here is a link to [Video Title]: [Link 1]

Here is a link to [Video Title]: [Link 2]

Let me know if you have a few minutes to learn more. Does next *Tuesday* at 2 PM work for you?

Thanks,
[Your Name]
[Contact Information]

4 FACEBOOK

The third aspect of the Digital Trifecta makes your brand bigger, gets you noticed more, and enhances your previous work. By tailoring your Facebook advertising to your custom audience, you will be able to touch each user approximately 60 times in month with ads running two to three times each day. You may think this is an aggressive tactic, but given the amount of advertising that inundates the average person on a daily basis, this is your way to compete with the big budgets of major corporations. You are working smarter.

"Work like there is someone working 24-hours a day to take it away from you."

– Mark Cuban

This quote has been following me for more than seven years and has a deeply personal meaning. While some may interpret Mark Cuban's words to mean that you should dedicate your life to work, he means the exact opposite. That is the definition of working smarter. The goal is to be ahead of those working 24 hours, not to join them. Your innovations will force them to work to catch up with you. You are not working to take anything from anyone. By using the Digital Trifecta, you are working to carve out your space as a small business entrepreneur in a world of conglomerates. Working around the clock is not the answer. Remaining practical and resourceful is.

Television advertising dominates the landscape and has been coupled with social media advertising. Why should you and your business be excluded? We are conditioned to expect the same consistent content from businesses on the platforms that we use the most. Your audience has been with you on the journey from LinkedIn to email to Facebook, and they will be impressed by your growth. They will not feel pressured to purchase your product, they will instead understand that you are exposing your brand and engaging with existing and potential customers.

Your presence is growing among your audience and beyond, as you are reaching people in both their personal and business worlds. LinkedIn is a touch during work hours, email is a touch whenever they prefer to use it, and Facebook is touch in their downtime. They are seeing you every day and in the first month, potentially 75 times in total across all platforms.

The Digital Trifecta is a path you and the user will travel together from an advertisement to a lead generation form and finally a conversion. Facebook has the ability to connect leads to almost any CRM which allows the easy management of leads. But if you do not have a CRM, that is not a problem as Facebook has its own Small Business CRM called "Facebook Lead Center". Facebook's Lead Center is a lead management tool that helps your business organize and maintain your customer contact information. Within the Center, you can easily organize, manage, and re-engage with your leads directly from your Facebook Business Page. Leads that are generated in Messenger are not yet supported. For example, maybe you have been keeping your lead contact information from your Lead Ads in a spreadsheet saved on your Desktop. With the Leads Center, leads that are acquired from your Lead Ads will automatically be added into the Leads Center. You can also import your own leads from a spreadsheet, or manually add new leads in one by one.

Selling becomes easier as you progress through the cycle of the Trifecta because your prospect is not only going to identify you by name, but they are also going to identify the company you represent, and the product you are selling. If they need your product, the sale is inevitable.

The Digital Trifecta relies on the principles of standard demand generation. Customer awareness, knowledge, and interest translated into conversations with consideration intent. This is relationship management in the digital age. Hustle and work ethic cannot be replaced by the tools at your disposal. Instead, the tools enhance your ability to automate repetition and track your progress in real-time. Satisfied customers will grow your business through loyalty referrals, endorsements, advocacy, and evangelism.

Process of matching customers from LinkedIn to Facebook

Like almost every small business I have worked with, the common trend has been "I tried Facebook, but it didn't work". And if you implemented the ads yourself, you are probably right, it likely didn't. The common trend with the businesses I have worked with is typically related to the business owner or their teenage child running their Facebook ads. This is exactly why the success rate is low. In order to have a successful campaign you need to ensure you are following the practices of your largest competitor, who is either using a seasoned social media marketer or an agency. But don't worry, I am going to spoil their secrets to improve your results.

First step is to ensure you have a Facebook Business Manager Account. Business Manager allows advertisers to manage their marketing efforts in one place and share access to assets across their team, partner agencies, and vendors. This process takes about 20-30 minutes to set up but allows you to maximize and analyze your results. If you already have a business manager, then you are ahead of the game, and can skip through this next section on the setup.

Facebook Setup

The setup process is simple. Follow these steps to get started.

1. Go to business.facebook.com/create and select Create Account.
2. Enter your name and confirm your identity with Facebook login credentials.
3. Follow the prompts to create your business account.

Business user set-up

1. Go to Settings - People and Assets - People.
2. Assign authorized agents to Ad Accounts and Pages with the appropriate role permissions.
3. Go to Business Settings - Instagram Accounts to connect any Instagram business accounts.
4. Add at least two people as Business Manager Admins and add the rest as Business Manager Employees.
5. Go to Pages - Add New Pages - Claim a Page to connect your Facebook Page. If you are a Page Admin your claim will be instantly approved. If you are not a Page Admin, a notification to approve the claim request will be sent to the

current Page Admin.
6. Go to Ad Accounts - Add new Ad Account. You will have the access to add an account you own by supplying the ad account ID, or request access to use another Business Manager owned ad account. Ad Account should be owned by the entity that pays invoices.

Setting up payment methods

Payment methods are required to create ads on Facebook. Follow these steps for assigning payment methods when you first set up your Business Manager.

1. Add the payment methods you want to use in Business Settings - Payments - Add Payment Method.
2. If you are eligible for a line of credit, check if your credit line is available in Business Manager. You can do this by reaching out to your Facebook sales rep or by visiting facebook.com/business/resources and selecting the Billing and Payments topic.
3. Define permissions levels in the Finance Roles section. Choose Finance Editor for those who will need to access credit lines or invoice details and choose Finance Analyst for those who will only need to view the information.
4. Go to Business Manager - People and select the person who needs the role.
5. Select the edit icon next to the person's name. In the dialog box under Finance Role, make the appropriate selection.

6. Update email addresses that need to receive invoices in Payments - Account Credit - Invoice Emails.
7. View Unpaid Delivery (balance) of credit line and general health in Settings - Payments.
8. Share your credit line to other Business Managers that need to access it, such as agencies.

After you have completed the initial setup for payment methods, you can create ad accounts and assign payment methods and lines of credit to them as needed, on a day-to-day basis.

Creating Custom Audiences

Now that your business manager setup is complete, it is time to implement the Facebook component of the Digital Trifecta by matching prospects from your LinkedIn account. As mentioned in the email section, the platform SalesQL is a huge component of identifying the details of your customer base. There are a few competitors of SalesQL, but this is where I have found the most success. To complete the process, you will need to export your contacts from your SalesQL dashboard and create a custom audience in Facebook.

To successfully match your LinkedIn contacts in Facebook, you need to upload a minimum of three personal identifiers (name, email & phone). You can also follow this process to target your existing customer base. Custom Audiences can help you reach your campaign objectives, but the security of the customer information you use is critical. Information you share with Facebook is hashed, that is, turned into short fingerprints that are impossible to reverse. This will ultimately protect the information you upload. Like the business manager section, if you already know how to create a Custom Audience, feel free to skip the next section on the setup process.

Below is the process to create the custom audience:

Let's take a look at how you can create a Lookalike Audience.

1. In the Audience section, below Custom Audiences, select **Create New.**
2. Choose **Lookalike Audience** from the dropdown.
3. Choose your source.
4. A source can be a Custom Audience that was not created using your pixel data, mobile app data or fans of your Page.
5. Consider using a group of 1,000 to 50,000 of your best customers based on lifetime value, transaction value, total order size or engagement.
6. Choose the country or countries where you'd like to find a similar set of people.
7. Choose your desired audience size using the slider.
8. Select **Create Audience.**
9. Select **Done.**

It may take six to 24 hours for your Lookalike Audience to be created. After that, it'll refresh every three to seven days as long as it's being used in an active ad set. You don't need to wait for a lookalike audience to update to use it for ad targeting. Now that you have the audience set up, it is time to start creating the ads!

Facebook Ad Set Creation

In this section, you will learn the most touch points of the Digital Trifecta. To have the most success it is critical that you utilize the Facebook Lead Generation campaign creation. Below are some of the critical components of Ad Set creation for this process.

1. Sign-in to "Facebook Business Manager" and click "+ Create" in the top left corner.
2. Buying Type: "Auction"
3. Consideration: "Lead Generation"
4. For the Trifecta, my recommendation is a $10-15 daily spend. This should/can be increased on a weekly basis by 20%. Do not jump more than 20% on a weekly basis as it will negatively impact your campaign results.
5. Ad Set: Select "Custom Audiences" and input your recently uploaded LinkedIn list.

The rest of the Ad Set creation is simple, but not complete. Following this section, you will see a series of ad examples that I have used for my customers who have had great results. But to execute these results you need to ensure you properly create your lead generation form. When creating your business's ad, select "**Create Form**". My recommendation is to keep this form as simple as possible, the less information you require, the more leads you will get. Facebook has a way to prepopulate the standard personal identifiers (name, email, city and phone). When building your first campaign, this is my immediate recommendation as you already know the target is in your demographic (heck, you can even cross-reference from LinkedIn). If you would like to gather additional information such as budget or area of interest, then this is OK but you will need to limit to no more than two additional questions.

Once your ad is created and running, these leads will be accessible in the Facebook Lead Center which can be accessed from your Facebook page. Since lead center is currently only available on desktop, I have been working with the mobile app "Privyr" which allows you to receive ALL of your Facebook leads directly to your phone. This app is extremely convenient and allows push notifications, so you never miss a lead. For a monthly charge of $18, you can have all your leads managed in one place and easily utilize the app to trigger SMS messages and email responses.

Now for what many of you might be

wondering, how do you build an engaging advertisement? I will share a series of my campaign secrets, but before I do, I want to share an extremely valuable tip. The big brand competition is spending in the tens of thousands to run social media campaigns. They are hiring teams both small and large, maybe even retaining agencies with them. So, why is this important? Well, it is simple, what if you could do what they are doing without trial and error? The cool thing is you can!

In 2018, Facebook faced a huge backlash following the Cambridge Analytica controversy of users' data being sold for the purposes of political advertising. This was chronicled in the Netflix documentary *The Great Hack*. This was especially disheartening considering that many users believe social media is (or at least should be) both authentic and transparent. When it is, it is actually a huge help to small businesses (and some have no idea). If you go to your competitors' Facebook page, and scroll to the bottom, (Ctrl+F "Transparency), you will be able to see every active advertisement run by your competitor.

Disclaimer: I am NOT telling you to steal their ads (you will likely violate policies). But what I AM telling you is to save time on searching for the perfect image or headline by getting ideas from your competition who has already done the heavy lifting. My goal has always been to do what the competition is doing, but better...much better. You know your audience, so take ideas from the competitor and adjust. But wait there's more!

When you see my ads, you will notice a common trend which revolves around credibility. The most successful ads of my competitors use words to establish "TRUST". Yes, this is the most successful word in each of my clients' ads. "Trust, Trusted, Trusted Partner, Trusted in XXX". It is simple, you need to build "Trust" with your ad. So "trust" me, these ads will take your campaign to the next level.

"A Brand is simply trust" – Steve Jobs

Facebook Ad Examples

Example #1: Security Camera Partner

Primary Text:
[Company Name] is a trusted security company that empowers thousands of IT departments worldwide to do more with less by redesigning video security from the ground up to be intuitive for anyone to use, effortless to maintain (No NVRs), infinitely scalable (Plug & Play), and secure by default (Encryption & outbound-only connections and more).

Headline:
Strengthen Security, Simplify Ownership

Description:
Connect all [Company] devices to Command, a web-based platform that makes it simple to manage devices at scale.

Example #2: Commercial Landscaping

Primary Text:
Your trusted Peekskill Landscaping Company. Our goal is to provide high-quality service for your commercial space!

Headline:
Your trusted Peekskill Commercial Landscaping Co.

Description:
We provide high-quality landscaping services

Example #3: Power Washing Company

Primary Text:
Your trusted Philadelphia Power Washing Partner. Regardless of if your needs are residential, or commercial, you can always trust us to provide high-quality service!

Headline:
Your trusted Philadelphia Power Washing Company.

Description:
High-quality power washing service

Example #4: Patient Management System

Primary Text:
Want to better manage your patients? [Company Name] has been providing business solutions for over 30 years. Let us make your process more cost efficient!

Headline:
[Company Name] Patient Monitoring System

Description:
A trusted partner simplifying the patient management process

5 THE DIGITAL TRIFECTA & YOU

Paid, owned, and earned media are tried and historically classified aspects of digital media. These will be woven into and utilized by The Digital Trifecta. Paid media within the Digital Trifecta will apply only to your Facebook advertising. Beyond your success with the Trifecta or perhaps even before, you will have developed a brand presence through a variety of outlets.

Your owned media will be everything that you bring to the table in relation to your brand and the Digital Trifecta. Your profile is your most important asset.

Most professionals are familiar with the Myers-Briggs report and the many variations that helped spawn an entire industry around coaching, leadership, and personal well-being. At the highest level, the Myers-Briggs identifies whether you are an introvert or an extrovert. Neither is a hindrance to the Trifecta and whatever your type, you can adjust accordingly.

For instance, if you are a natural introvert, the idea of outreach can be daunting. However, consider the fact that you are working in a digital medium and you are using the Trifecta tools to engage with people daily. You can tailor the process to your personal preferences while keeping to the basic outline for success.

If you are an extrovert, connecting with individuals is the easy part. However, you must remain conscious that there is work to do beyond selling. The data and details needed to complete the Trifecta should not be overshadowed by your charisma and drive.

Networking is essential to continued success in any field. A robust web of individuals willing to buy, sell, and promote your products are invaluable to your future business. Organic growth is inevitable when using The Digital Trifecta.

Remember, the Digital Trifecta is a roadmap designed to bring your best skills to light. You are the driving force behind the work and the reason for the success.

The elements available to you in The Digital Trifecta will build you beyond your business. Approaching LinkedIn first thing in the morning is an exercise in a healthy routine and a great way to challenge yourself by taking initiative. As your contact list grows and people begin reaching out to you, your responsiveness and availability will become appealing to them. When you take the steps to build your email campaigns, you are sharpening your creative and strategic skills. On Facebook, those skills are intensified by consistency.

When you wake up each day and sign-in to your LinkedIn profile, you are entering a realm filled with potential clients and competitors. With broad access to an international network of associates, you will not be the first person attempting to make a connection nor will you be the last. That 50% or less success rate that we previously discussed may not sound appealing and can even feel disheartening. This is only because we are often conditioned to believe that anything less than perfection is unworthy of praise. Even a 25% success rate will elevate your brand and generate revenue for your business - new revenue! The fear of rejection is real, and for some people, it can be a deterrent to taking risks. Consider reframing that fear as understanding that the only loss in this situation is a missed opportunity. A lack of response or a firm "no" from someone you have attempted is not a setback. Rather, it is a clear motivator to continue working and connecting.

6 FOSTERING THE RELATIONSHIP

Business, much like life, relies on relationship-building skills to achieve happiness. The Digital Trifecta modifies some of the steps you would take to build a personal connection, but at its core, it remains the same. The Internet provides you with the opportunity to efficiently connect with multiple individuals. While in-person contacts require you to introduce yourself to one person or a small group at a time, you are beginning this process by connecting with 50 people daily. However, making the connection, learning about these new contacts, and self-disclosing are all essential for success.

We build relationships for a variety of reasons: friendship, networking, partnership, etc. The added component resulting from The Digital Trifecta is business growth. Authenticity is still required, which makes this the perfect tool for a small business. You will be able to connect quickly with individuals on a national and international scale while maintaining the bandwidth to engage personally with those in your immediate area. Your contacts will be growing through social media, but a great way to build relationships is to support the causes or events hosted by your potential client's company when you are both interested.

A post-COVID world will challenge us to step out of our comfort zones and choose to use the tools we were forced to use during the pandemic. Community is essential to progress, and building one virtually - filled with individuals focused on their definition of success - will increase your chances for positive results.

While following the Digital Trifecta, practicing self-awareness is key to managing rejection and staying focused. As mentioned earlier, the conversion rate from contact to customer may be less than 50%. Depending on your field, the success rate may be 25%. Keep pushing and keep putting yourself out there. Your connections who convert will become your contacts. They believe in your product and more importantly, they believe in you. Your work ethic and presence online led to a purchase, but it is their admiration for you that has put them into a recurring cycle.

Achieving the goal of conversion to a one-time or repeat customer is a matter of recurring visibility. "Absence makes the heart grow fonder" is one relationship adage that does not apply to business. Through the Digital Trifecta you will develop a steady flow of frequency of contact. In doing so, your customers and potential customers become accustomed to hearing from you on certain days at certain times. Navigating the digital space does not eliminate the human tendency to be creatures of habit. Instead, it provides us with more chances to develop new ones, learn new skills, and open ourselves to more opportunities.

7 A Universal Solution

The Digital Trifecta is a universal solution. It is applicable to any sector and scalable for any business. Each component within the Trifecta is available to you and free to acquire. But remember: the most important aspect is you. Your decision whether to use these tools will define your business in a digital world. Using your personal touch while navigating the digital landscape can put you in stadiums, on billboards, and across mass media. You will define what success means to you. Most importantly, you are building relationships and your business simultaneously to fulfill whatever your dream may be.

Your relationships with technology, business, finances, and others all factor into the use of the Trifecta. Those same relationships will multiply daily. The addition of individuals to the outreach, communication, and conversion cycles pays dividends both tangible and intangible. The effects of the Digital Trifecta will be seen in the trends of your email opens, Facebook views, online interactions, and your bottom line. Throughout this book, I have given away my process. They are open secrets. Whether you are an entrepreneur or an entrepreneurial sales lead in a major company, The Digital Trifecta is at your fingertips and leverages your place in a world where bloated marketing budgets and minimal creativity dominate the market. With three steps, you create endless opportunities.

The Internet is the most powerful utility in the digital world and smartphones are the fastest growing technologies in history. We are connected to one another across countries and time zones. Competition is a reality, but collaboration is more common, and it begins with contact. Success with The Digital Trifecta will put eyes on you, but instead of blindly attempting to reach them all, you get to choose who will be looking back.

Enjoy the book? Please share your feedback on social media and be sure to tag me!

https://www.linkedin.com/in/frankmazza1/

https://www.facebook.com/FrankMazzaIII/

https://twitter.com/frankmazza3

https://www.instagram.com/frankmazza3/

www.ingramcontent.com/pod-product-compliance
Lightning Source LLC
Chambersburg PA
CBHW070837220526
45466CB00002B/804